**Understanding
My Emotions**

When I'm Happy

Understanding My Emotions

When I'm Angry
When I'm Embarrassed
When I'm Happy
When I'm Lonely
When I'm Overwhelmed
When I'm Sad
When I'm Scared
When I'm Sorry
When I'm Surprised
When I'm Worried

Understanding My Emotions

When I'm Happy

ALEXANDRA DALTON

**Understanding My Emotions
When I'm Happy**

Copyright © 2016 by Village Earth Press, a division of Harding House Publishing. All rights reserved. No part of this publication may be reproduced or transmitted in any form or by any means, electronic or mechanical, including photocopying, recording, taping, or any information storage and retrieval system, without permission from the publisher.

Village Earth Press
Vestal, New York 13850
www.villageearthpress.com

First Printing
9 8 7 6 5 4 3 2 1

Series ISBN (paperback): 978-1-62524-440-6
ISBN (paperback): 978-1-62524-378-2
ebook ISBN: 978-1-62524-134-4
   Library of Congress Control Number: 2014944100

Author: Dalton, Alexandra.

Contents

To the Teacher or Parent	7
When I'm Happy	8
Find Out More	42
Feeling Words	44
Index	46
Picture Credits	47
About the Author	48

To the Teacher or Parent

More than a hundred years ago, John Dewey insisted that the true purpose of schooling was not simply to teach children a trade but to train them in deeper habits of mind. Social-emotional learning builds on Dewey's theory further, suggesting that emotional skills are crucial to both academic performance and future success in life.

The research is definitive: emotional training is good for children! A recent study, reported in the *New York Times,* found that preschoolers who had even a single year of social-emotional training continued to perform better two years after they left the program; they were less aggressive and less anxious than children who hadn't participated in the program. Another study found that K-12 students who received some form of emotional instruction scored an average of 11 percentile points higher on standardized achievement tests. A similar study found a nearly 20 percent decrease in students' violent behaviors.

The goal of this series of books, UNDERSTANDING MY EMOTIONS, is to instill in young children a foundation of emotional intelligence. Use these books to help children learn to understand, identify, and regulate their emotions. Give them important tools that will serve them well for the rest of their lives!

When I'm Happy

When I'm happy, I feel something inside me. It's a good feeling. It's just one of lots of feelings I have inside me.

The feelings I have inside me are called emotions. They come and they go. Sometimes I feel good and sometimes I feel bad.

My feelings come partly from whatever is happening around me. They come from things that are going on INSIDE me too. If I'm hungry or I'm sleepy, I get upset more easily. If I'm getting a cold or I have a stomachache, I might not feel happy.

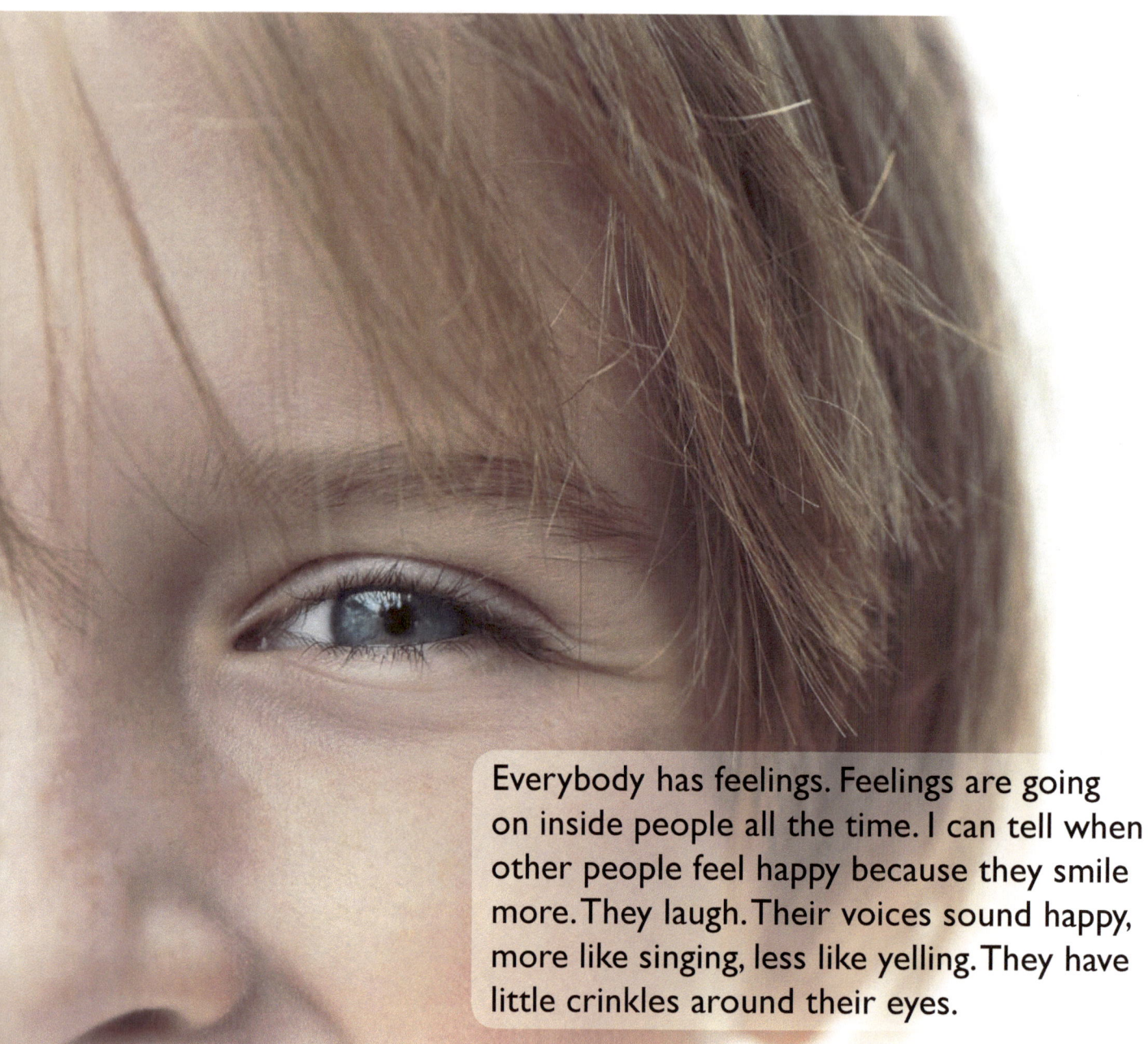

Everybody has feelings. Feelings are going on inside people all the time. I can tell when other people feel happy because they smile more. They laugh. Their voices sound happy, more like singing, less like yelling. They have little crinkles around their eyes.

When I'm happy, I tell other people too. I use my face, my body, and my voice to let others know that I'm feeling happy.

No one feels happy all the time.

Sometimes people feel sad.

Sometimes they feel scared.

Sometimes they feel angry.

Sometimes they just feel bored!

These are all different kinds of emotions. That's just the way life is.

Emotions take place inside people. I can't see exactly what other people are feeling, but I can usually tell when people are sad or angry, scared or bored. Their mouths and eyebrows give me clues about what they're feeling.

The way they move and hold their bodies give me more clues. If I pay attention to these clues, I can look at people and see how they're feeling. I can understand them. And sometimes THAT makes me happy!

Lots of different things make me happy. I feel happy inside when I get a birthday present.

My best friend makes me happy.

I also feel happy when I'm swimming.

I feel happy when I play with my dog.

I'm happy when I'm with the people who love me.

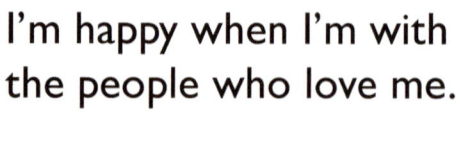

And sometimes acting silly makes me feel happy!

Slides and balls make me happy!

Birthday parties are happy times too.

Being with people makes me happy sometimes—but other times, I'm happy when I'm all by myself.

Reading makes me happy.

I feel happy when I'm alone watching the sun set.

Using my hands to do and make things almost always makes me happy.

I feel happy when I draw a picture.

Or when I make music.

I feel happy when I finger paint!

I feel happy when I'm in my favorite outdoor spot.

I feel happy when I run!

Sometimes, I'm happy for no real reason at all. I just feel happy!

I don't always feel happy, though. Now and then, I feel the opposite of happy. I feel sad! When I'm sad, my face tells others people what I'm feeling. I have a sad face, just like I have a happy face.

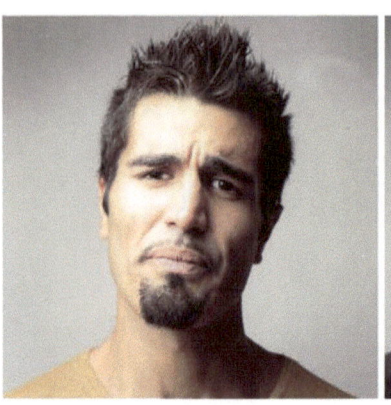 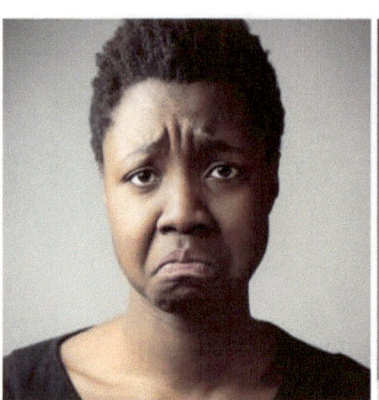 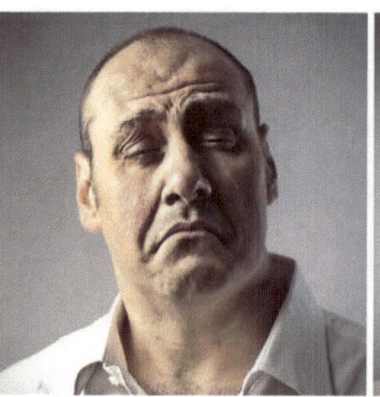 

I can tell that other people are sad the same way—their faces tell me they are sad. Their voices and their bodies say they're sad.

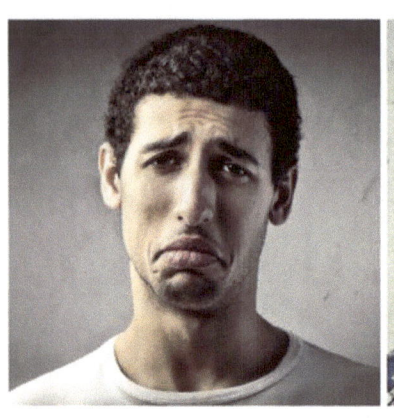  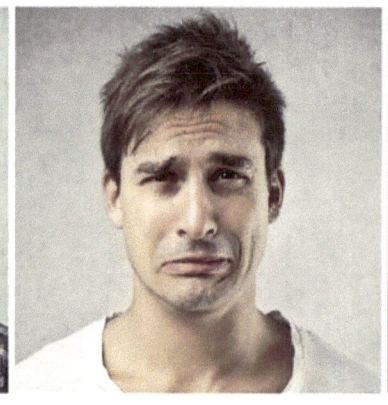 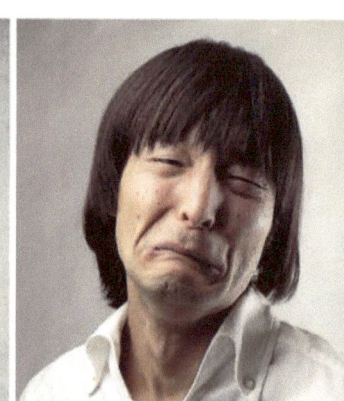

They don't have to use words to tell me. I just know by looking at them!

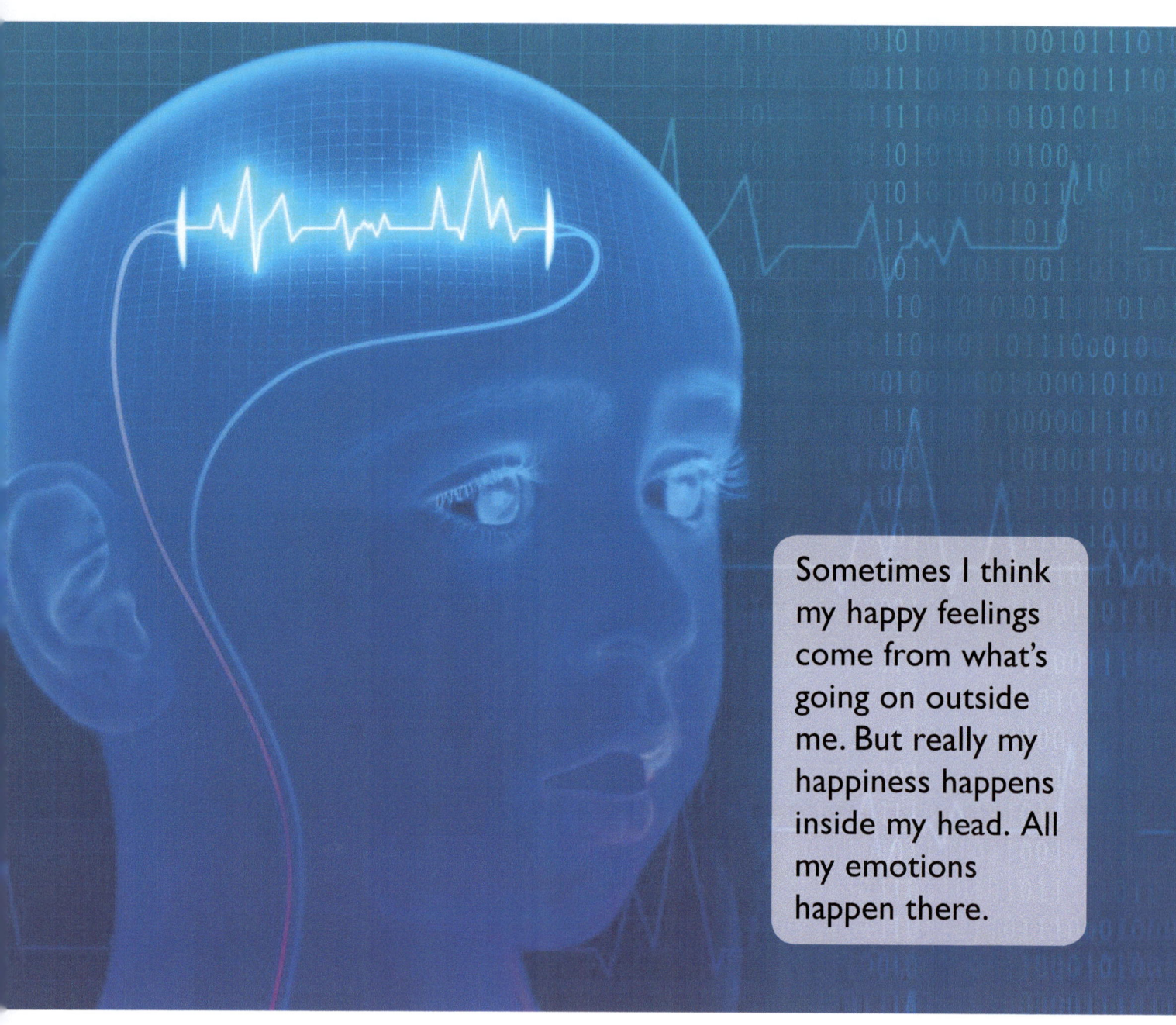

Sometimes I think my happy feelings come from what's going on outside me. But really my happiness happens inside my head. All my emotions happen there.

Inside my head is my brain. My brain looks like this. You can't see my brain, of course, because it's inside me, where no one can see it. But my brain is what gives me my emotions.

When I feel happy, it's like a message from my brain. The message says,

"Pay attention! Something good is happening! Try to get more of this in your life, because this is a good thing!"

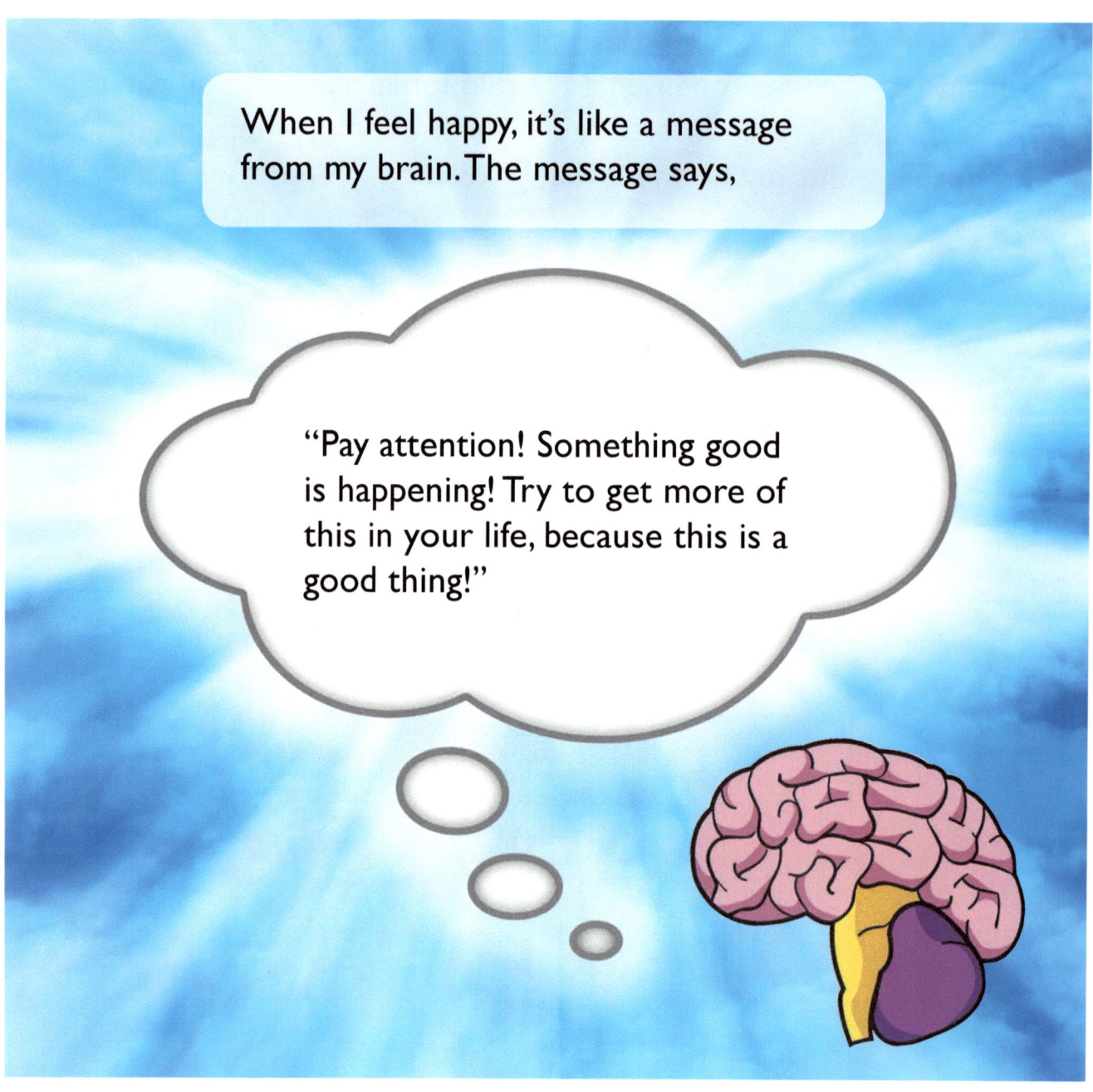

I can listen to my happy feelings. Then I know what to do to make myself happy the next time I'm feeling sad.

I can't help feeling sad sometimes. But when I do, I can cheer myself up by doing something that makes me happy, like blowing bubbles.

I can decide to think happy thoughts instead of sad thoughts. I can decide to smile instead of frown!

I can't help feeling sad sometimes. But when I do, I can cheer myself up by doing something that makes me happy.

When I'm worried or scared, thinking happy thoughts helps me feel better. When I'm angry, doing happy things calms me down.

I'm NEVER bored when I'm doing the things that make me happy!

Here are some of the things I do when I'm sad to cheer me up:

I talk to someone who loves me.

I play hide-and-go-seek with my friends.

I give someone a hug.

I build something, even something little!

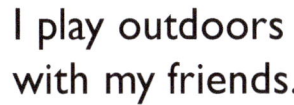

I play outdoors with my friends.

That's what makes ME happy. What about you?

What makes YOU happy?

Find Out More

You can learn more about your emotions by going online and checking out these websites. Some of the sites have videos you can watch or games you can play. You could also read the other books in this series to find out more about feelings—or you could go to your library and see if you can find the books listed on the next page. There's a lot more you can learn about feelings!

On the Internet

Happy, Mad, Silly, Sad
pbskids.org/barney/children/games/happymadgame.html

It's My Life: Emotions
pbskids.org/itsmylife/emotions

KidsHealth: Feelings
kidshealth.org/kid/feeling

Model Me: Faces and Emotions
www.modelmekids.com/emotions_dvd.html

In Books

Aliki. *Feelings*. New York: Greenwillow Books, 2007.

Cain, Janan. *The Way I Feel*. Seattle, Wash.: Parenting Press, 2000.

Curtis, Jamie Lee. *Today I Feel Silly: And Other Moods That Make My Day*. New York: HarperCollins, 2007.

Emberley, Ed and Anne Miranda. *Glad Monster, Sad Monster: A Book About Feelings*. New York: Little Brown, 2007.

Freyman, Saxton. *How Are You Peeling?* Danbury, Conn.: Scholastic, 2004.

Krueger, David. *What Is a Feeling?* Seattle, Wash.: Parenting Press, 2013.

Rotner, Shelley. *Lots of Feelings*. Minneapolis, Minn.: Millbrook Press, 2003.

Snow, Todd. *Feelings to Share from A to Z*. Lake Elmo, Minn.: Maren Green, 2007.

Feeling Words

Happy and sad are two of the words we use when we talk about feelings. But there are many more words that describe feelings. Here are some of those words.

Excited

Angry

Embarrassed

Lonely

Guilty

Hurt

Proud

Scared

Shy

Sorry

Surprised

Worried

Index

An index is a way you can quickly find something inside a book. The numbers tell you exactly what page to go to if you want to find that word.

angry 15, 16, 36, 44

birthday 21
body 13, 29
bored 15, 16, 37
brain 31, 32

dog 19
draw 24

embarrassed 44
emotions 10, 15, 31
eyebrows 16
eyes 12

face 13, 27
feelings 9, 11, 12
finger paint 24
friend 18, 38, 39

frown 34

guilty 44

hands 24
happy 9, 12, 13, 17–26, 32–36, 40, 41
head 30, 31
hug 39
hungry 11
hurt 44

lonely 44
love 20, 38

mouths 16

outdoors 25, 38

play 38, 39
proud 45

sad 14, 16, 27–29, 33
scared 14, 16, 36, 45
shy 45
silly 21
sleepy 11
surprised 45
swimming 19
stomachache 11

thoughts 34

voice 13, 29

worried 36, 45

Picture Credits

p. 8 © Miroslav Ferkuniak | Dreamstime.com
p. 9 © Miroslav Ferkuniak | Dreamstime.com
p. 10 © Miroslav Ferkuniak | Dreamstime.com
p. 11 © Miroslav Ferkuniak | Dreamstime.com
p. 12 © Gillian08 | Dreamstime.com
p. 13 © Miroslav Ferkuniak | Dreamstime.com
p. 14 © Yelena Rodriguez | Dreamstime.com, © Godfer | Dreamstime.com
p. 15 © Phovoir | Dreamstime.com, © Jason Stitt | Dreamstime.com
pp. 16–17 Fotolia: © Konovalov, © Igor Mojzes
p. 18 © Kenneth Sponsler | Dreamstime.com © Jarenwicklund | Dreamstime.com
p. 19 © Micaela Sanna | Dreamstime.com, © Miroslav Ferkuniak | Dreamstime.com
p. 20 © Miroslav Ferkuniak | Dreamstime.com
p. 21 Fotolia: © JDavenport85, Blend Images
p. 22 © Miroslav Ferkuniak | Dreamstime.com
p. 23 © Jose Manuel Gelpi Diaz | Dreamstime.com, © Jo Ann Snover | Dreamstime.com
p. 24 © Elena Rostunova | Dreamstime.com , © Atm2003 | Dreamstime.com, © Picsfive | Dreamstime.com
p. 25 © Miroslav Ferkuniak | Dreamstime.com

p. 26 © Miroslav Ferkuniak | Dreamstime.com
p. 27 © Miroslav Ferkuniak | Dreamstime.com
pp. 28–29 Fotolia: © Olly
p. 30 © Grafoo | Dreamstime.com
p. 31 © Kts | Dreamstime.com
p. 32 © Mishkacz | Dreamstime.com, © Paulvg | Dreamstime.com
p. 33 © Miroslav Ferkuniak | Dreamstime.com
p. 34 © Lauratran | Dreamstime.com
p. 35 © Stephen Coburn | Dreamstime.com
p. 36 © Denys Kuvaiev | Dreamstime.com
p. 37 © Miroslav Ferkuniak | Dreamstime.com
p. 38 © Miroslav Ferkuniak | Dreamstime.com
p. 39 © Miroslav Ferkuniak | Dreamstime.com, © Julija Sapic | Dreamstime.com, © Zurijeta | Dreamstime.com
p. 40 © Miroslav Ferkuniak | Dreamstime.com
p. 41 © Monkey Business Images | Dreamstime.com
p. 44 Fotolia: © Fasphotographic, © Cantor Pannato, © Andres Rodriguez, © Gabriel Blaj, © Moodboard Premium, © Halfpoint
p. 45 Fotolia: © Cantor Pannato, © Blend Images, © Zhekos, © Olly, © Wavebreak Media Micro, © Muro

About the Author

Alexandra Dalton was a teacher, and now she is a writer. When she was a teacher, she helped her students talk about their feelings. She knows that it's hard work sometimes to talk about our feelings—but she knows we feel better and we get along with each other better when we can use our words to talk about how we feel. Alexandra has three children. She also has a dog and a cat and four goats. She lives in New York State.

www.ingramcontent.com/pod-product-compliance
Lightning Source LLC
Chambersburg PA
CBHW061359090426
42743CB00002B/68